Ibiza.

Ibiza has drawn free minds for decades. And the magnetism that has attracted people like Walter Benjamin, Roger Waters and the harbingers of hippy culture over the years still glows in the sand of the isle.

The Ibizan club scene exploded in the 1990s, but beyond the super DJs, there's a year-round community of creative internationals weaving a vital scene. Off-season and on-, visitors can discover stunning natural trails and villages suspended in time, eclectic live music experiences, a growing contemporary art scene and a fantastic array of fresh restaurants.

In Ibiza, LOST iN spoke to a music promoter and fashion designer couple, a curator of a forward-thinking art space, a private chef and cookbook writer, a rambler who knows the magical corners of the island and a pioneer who has helped shaped the clubbing scene since the 1970s. A journalist explores the changing myths surrounding Es Vedrà, the transcendental rock that's provided inspiration for centuries, while a photo showcase highlights the golden era of Ibiza's hippy chic. It's all about original minds and the creative vibe. Get lost in the sights, sounds and flavours of the island. Get lost in Ibiza.

Some say it was a Phoenician quarry, others that it provided sandstone for Ibiza's walls in the 16th century. Whatever its origins, carved faces, gods and monsters testify to *Sa Pedrera de Cala d'Hort's* discovery by hippies in the 1960s—who named it *Atlantis*. Today it's a spectacular trip for those in shape enough to make it back up. Drive from Es Cubells to Cala d'Hort, and turn left onto a dirt track. Park and descend on foot to the sunken city.

Atlantis (Sa Pedrera de Cala d'Hort), Sant Josep

Time Capsule

When you open a box of old photos or childhood toys it can trigger a strange transportation. Stepping into the time capsule that is the Ibizan village of *Sant Agustí* might spark a slightly different process. But though you have no memories of living in the 300-year-old village, somehow you can feel exactly what it was like back then. Now, there's plenty of time to admire how beautiful it all is. The church, the surrounding Sant Josep mountains, the white and the blue... And the friendly people happy enough to live in that monument to the beauty of simplicity.
• Sant Agustí des Vedrà, Sant Josep

From Conceptual Art to Botiga Blues

Inspiration Island

Food Hidden Pleasures

Imagine you get fired from a Michelin-starred restaurant in Copenhagen—and then another one. After that you open an illegal food club in your home, get busted and evicted. What do you do? You open a hidden seven-table high-end Nordic-cuisine restaurant in an Eivissa no-go area, with a big steel door to keep your guests safe—if they make it that far, that is. Well, that's what Boris Buono did. And what LOST iN will do is endorse *Ibiza Food Studio* with that story alone—without even telling you how special the food is. Reserve via Facebook.
• Ibiza Food Studio, Eivissa

Artful Island

The recent spike in Ibiza's art credentials owes in no small part to the efforts of billionaire Cirque du Soleil founder Guy Laliberté. He set up exhibition space *Lune Rouge*—in a former industrial area close to the port—principally to showcase his own extensive, and growing, collection. The adjoining *Art Projects Ibiza* is backed by prestigious global gallerists Blum & Poe, and has hosted hulking names such as Cindy Sherman, Takashi Murakami and Jenny Holzer, working closely with the artists and local artisans to produce commissioned projects with a local flavour. If your retinas are burned out from sunsets, these spaces could provide some more conceptual fodder.
• Art Projects Ibiza + Lune Rouge, Eivissa, artprojectsibiza.com

Queen Beach

Thanks to the filtering activities of local aquatic flora Posidonia, the Ibizan sea is as clear and crystalline as can be. And there's a beach to suit every fancy. The geological wonder of Sant Antoni's *Punta Galera* (pictured) presents layered flat rocks and optimal sunbathing turf, plus the occasional hidden mojito stand and unparalleled sunsets. Serene little *Cala Xuclar* (Sant Joan), meanwhile, requires less hiking and is ideal for sinking in the umbrella far from civilisation. At *Aguas Blancas* (Santa Eulària), still popular with nudists, a shallow walk into the water is friendly to kids, with cliffs jutting out dramatically above. Idyllic *Cala Salada* (Sant Antoni), a protected cove just north of Sant Antoni town, offers sandy shores for lounging and clear waters, surrounded by a rocky seabed rife with fauna. For busier days, the less-frequented Cala Saladeta, just over the rocks, is an excellent plan B.

• Various locations, see Index p. 63

Night | **Not for Everyone**

There was a time you'd walk back to your car from the beach to find a giant, cryptic "U" written in the red dust on your window. These invites are no longer used, but the slogan of nightclub *Underground* remains "Not For Everyone". In the woods just off the road in Sant Rafael, nights at "el Under" alternate between laid-back and throbbing, thanks to a rotating cast of big-name DJs eager to play alongside owner Juanito. The stronghold of underground club culture draws locals for their typical after-work caña.

• Underground, Sant Antoni, ibizaunderground.com

Food **Shore Thing**

Though seaside eating seldom disappoints, the memory of a handful of Ibiza's many beach restaurants will remain with you longer than your tan. At *El Bigotes*, off Cala Mastell (Santa Eulària), watch the fishermen bring in the catch for your meal. A specialty is Ibizan "bullit de peix", a fish stew served in three delicious parts. Near Eivissa, *El Chiringuito de María* (pictured) is ripe for any seafood lover. The bare-bones shack on the Sa Punta rocks serves the daily catch with salad and little else. It's a finer lunch at *Es Torrent* (Sant Josep), with a privileged view of cliffs from beneath the straw huts. Sip your claru and onjoy their famous "arroz a banda", or rice in fish stock.
• Various locations, see Index p. 63

Night **Roadside Jam**

In the olden days islanders would gather in "botigas"—grocery stores—to pass the time. One of few remaining is *Can Jordi Blues Station*. Not only can you buy basic foodstuffs alongside Ibiza specialties and drink at the bar, but you can also soak up exhibited art and—usually on weekend nights—catch live concerts that have become legendary. International musicians occasionally turn up alongside island greats for jam sessions before a devoted crowd. Rub shoulders with labourers and locals while sipping from a wide beer selection. Check the Facebook page for opportunities to enjoy the magic of this particular place.
• Can Jordi Blues Station, Sant Josep

Toby Clarke, Tour Guide

Roaming Wild

Emerson complained that the civilised man had built the coach but lost the use of his feet. Ibiza is the perfect place to plant these feet on solid ground and put them back to work. To give them some direction, we asked Walking Ibiza's Toby Clarke to map out the island for us

You grew up in Ibiza until you were ten, where did you live and how did the island change in the years you were forced away?

Forced away is very true. I grew up in a little suburb of Santa Eulària called Siesta. A beautiful little place, away from everything, very quiet and wonderful. These days my wife and me live in Sant Joan. The island has changed enormously since my childhood days. There are a lot more buildings now—mostly villas. Seldomly you find a beautiful hillside with nothing built on it anymore. But the island still has its beautiful essence. If you want to look for it and find it, the real Ibiza is still here, very much so in little villages like *Sant Carles, Santa Agnès* or *Sant Agustí*. These villages are still exactly the same as they've always been.

What does Ibiza mean to you?

Well, it's my home. I went away, because I thought I wanted to discover the world, the big city, the bright lights… But what I discovered was how important home to me is. I think for everybody home has a big pull back, especially when you had an amazing childhood like me.

So how did you come up with the idea of making hiking your passion and profession?

I didn't come up with the idea, it really came to me. When I came back to the island in 2009 I started doing various things, trying to figure out what I wanted to do in life. Then one day I came up with the idea of walking around the the island to see if it is possible to follow the whole coastline. To my knowledge, and I did a lot of research on it, no one else had ever done it. So the evening before I took off, I was trying to figure out

how to survive this trip, because it was the end of the season and only a few beach bars would be open. I had this epiphany to take only one euro with me. My wife was adamant that I at least take food and water with me for 24 hours. So I did that and off we went, me and my young dog Cosmo, trying to survive in the wild. And survive we did. We came back after 11 days and had survived on a lot of begging, borrowing, stealing and a lot of luck and trust that food will always come my way. And it did, everywhere I went, I got food. Although I did go hungry a few times, went very thirsty a few times and even had to teach Cosmo how to lick the morning dew from the leaves to get water.

Is all of Ibiza completely mapped out for you, or do you still find new adventures, new trails?

That's the one thing I am always amazed by on Ibiza. I know the island quite well, especially the coastline. I've walked it now four times and kayaked around most of it as well. But inland it's a mystery. You think you know an area and suddenly you come across a valley you didn't even know was there. You find new springs, new wonderful ruined fincas, farmhouses… So it's truly a magical island, where even in my own very close neighborhood I find trails I didn't know existed. I mix it up by taking the mountain bike to be faster and find more new places.

What would be the top hiking routes you'd recommend to Ibiza newbies?

One of my favourite hikes I do is called "The Lost City". This is midway down the west coast. When the Christians invaded the island in 1235, the Moors didn't want to fight them, because they'd heard of all the terrible things the

Thirty years of a practically unchanged menu keeps pulling people back to seaside Restaurante Sa Caleta

Christians would do to them if they resisted. So they left the Old Town of Ibiza and trekked across the island to Cap d'Albarca on the west coast, which must have been a humongous task back then, to set up their new home. And this time they built a wall around their city. The remains of that wall, a bit of an Ibizan equivalent to the Great Wall of China, still exist and set the scenery for a beautiful walk through the Lost City. Another hike that's quite popular is to *Atlantis (Sa Pedrera),* another lost city. When you get down there you'll know why people call that place Atlantis. There is a lot of sandstone and over the years people have carved out Buddhas and peace signs. It's quite a magical place. Another beautiful hike is to a place called *Es Broll.* It's an inland hike to the only spot on Ibiza that has all-year-long flowing water. It's in a valley, almost like in the French Alps. It has lots of olive trees, orange trees... A truly beautiful place.

What are Ibiza's most spectacular beaches?

Well, it depends on what you are looking for. In the beginning of the season, one of my favourites is *Cala Bassa* beach: a lovely white sandy beach with crystal blue water. Then *Es Portitxol* is another great one. You can only get there by hiking or by boat. It's a beautiful, C-shaped beach. It's so secluded that even if you go there in midsummer, there might be only three or four people on the whole beach. *Cala Comte* I also like a lot, but it gets really busy.

The winter blooming of the almond trees is spectacular. Do you ever get to harvest them?

Yeah the almonds blossomed very early this year, they came out full bloom in January. Absolutely spectacular. I did quite a few full-moon almond blossom walks. The best place to see them would be the Santa Agnès valley. I have harvested them in the past, but to crack open enough of them to actually make something is such a painstaking process, that it's not practical. And unbelievably there has only been an almond-cracking machine on the island since 2015. Before that there was none. One day I asked a farmer if he had an almond-cracking machine and he said yes. I said I'd never heard of someone who had one and I was born on the island. And he said, I have one, and she's actually doing it right now. He meant his grandmother… She was his almond-cracking machine.

How about the Ibiza wildlife? What would be a good hike to experience it?

The biggest wild animal Ibiza has is the rabbit, so that's as wild as you can get. But we do have a good amount of bird life. Lots of falcons, red kites, buzzards and the stunningly beautiful little hoopoe, which is a symbol of Ibiza. The best way to see falcons and buzzards is probably kayaking under caves or overhangs, where they like to nest. You can watch them fly in and out, but don't get too close.

So what are Ibiza's hidden treasures? Are there any myths and legends you'd like to share?

So while there are lot of Ibiza myths and legends, the biggest would be Es Vedrà, an island just off the south coast. This is said to be the third most magnetic point on the entire planet—after the North and South Poles. It's been disputed a bit recently, but my take is that history has shown that this place has always had a mystical draw towards it. One of the myths revolving around it, is that this was the island where the sirens wanted to steer Odysseus off course and into disaster.

So when you come back to civilisation, where do you treat yourself with a good meal?

The good thing about Ibiza is the yin and yang. You can have a great meal for 11 euros, or you can go to one of the posh beach houses and spend a thousand, if you have that kind of money. There is a great seafood restaurant near Portinatx called *S'illot de Rencli*. A good Spanish restaurant near Sant Joan would be *Can Curune*. They have a great meal of the day for 11 euros. It's a really friendly and tasty restaurant. Another great one is *Restaurant Es Cubells* right next to a church in the beautiful village with the same name. They make a great paella and amazing puddings. Another one of my favourites is *Bar Anita* in Sant Carles, a very traditional place—just because I was going there since I was in my mummy's tummy. They do a great dirty burger, which is great hangover food by the way. Then you have *Can Cosmi* in Santa Agnès, they do a great Spanish tortilla. I also like *The Giri Café*, run by very friendly Dutch people, with a nice, very modern decoration—a stark contrast when you go through its doors from the very old village. Great food, not expensive. And *Restaurant Sa Caleta* in Sant Josep is another lovely place to have fish.

Beyond the beaches: take in Ibiza's charming campo on one of Toby's walking tours

Time Trails

From secluded coves to forgotten villages, there's ample material for getting lost in the north of Ibiza. Let the dusty roads lead you to your destination, but don't forget to stop and smell the fig trees

Culture Night | Field Jam

Any rural Ibizan adventure would be incomplete without a visit to ad hoc wonderland *Tetra House*. The repurposed payesa house sits in a field surrounded by a greenhouse, workshops, exhibition spaces and the stage the resident collective of artists has set up as the venue for their weekly jam sessions. The musical soirées draw artists from all over and extend long into the night, providing a way for even seasoned islanders to still get lost in Ibiza. A modern hippy refuge, Tetra offers an authentic glimpse into what island life is like for some of the creative locals who live here. Aside from an entertaining alternative to the massive club night, the cultural centre also offers movie nights, workshops and the occasional lecture.

• Tetra, Santa Eulària, tetraibiza.com

Food	Rich Herbs

Local digestif hierbas ibicencas is found all over the island—but finding the finest requires some roaming. In the tranquil square of Sant Miquel Church, *Estanco Can Xicu* (Sant Joan) has held ground for 100 years. Thousands of boots continue to scuff the unchanged floor awaiting its lauded snuff. In Santa Eulària, *Bar Anita* (pictured) is another institution—plus a literal home address for some Ibizan locals. Since the 1960s it's been a favourite with artists, writers and hippies, who'd trade work for drink and excellent tapas. But what both places have in common is their hierbas—perhaps the best on the island.
• Various locations, see Index p. 63

Shop	Couture and Décor

Yvonne and Hans Nuyten at *Sluiz* (pictured) in Santa Gertrudis village are retail mavericks, to say the least. Their gigantic emporium, guarded by a flamboyant herd of sculpted cattle, houses a selection of clothing, homeware, food and curiosities. Furnishings and textiles come from independent designers as well as an in-house, locally made namesake label. Smaller in space, though not in substance, is another village resident *The Rose*. Along with clothing and homewares, find paintings by one owner Aldo Kodac and hand-sewn silk pieces designed by the other owner Claudina Damonte.
• Santa Eulària, various locations, see Index p. 63

Food	Bird of Paradise

This reconverted finca in the middle of the sleepy Sant Llorenc countryside is an oasis of colour, tastes and smells. Serving only cold dishes during the day and a fuller menu at night, *La Paloma* prides itself on preparing food with the utmost care, with ingredients sourced from their own garden and friends' farms both in Ibiza and Tuscany. Kids are welcome and the evenings have been known to turn into musical affairs. Come at noon for breathtaking views of the campo, or in the evening to try the homemade pasta, with plenty of options for vegans and bio-lovers.
• La Paloma, Sant Joan, palomaibiza.com

Olive Branch

In Sant Llorenç village, the old schoolhouse is today home to Ibiza's first "oleoteca". At *Ses Escoles*, the olive oil mill is accompanied by a rustic but elegant restaurant in which the interior design reflects the kitchen concept. Co-founder and chef Miguel Llabrés focuses on traditional Balearic cuisine with a modern twist. Naturally the three variations of house olive oil "Can Miquel Guasch" can be found on each table. On hot nights sit in the cosy inner yard.

• Ses Escoles, Sant Joan, canmiquelguasch.com

Shop **Time for Stalling**

Summer or winter, a Sunday best spent on Ibiza is at the *Sant Joan Market*. Every edge of the Plaza de España is lined with little stores helmed by local farmers selling their weekly yield of olives, bags of spices and bottles of the island's mighty liquor Hierbas Ibicencas. Local artisans fill the remaining space, offering everything from handcrafts and musical instruments to artworks and natural soaps. But, more than the goods on sale, it's the atmosphere that makes the visit worthwhile. An authentic community vibe makes for a humble taste of Ibiza.

• Sant Joan Market, Sant Joan

Outdoors **Tranquil Oasis**

Although Ibiza is famous for its hippies and beaches, you don't have to rough it on the wellness stakes. *Atzaró Spa* belongs to a luxury agro-tourism complex situated in a century-old farm but open to the public. Swim in the 43-metre long outdoor pool, sweat in the hammam, work out in the gym or relax with massages. All the facilities are embedded in a huge Mediterranean garden among Ibizan architecture. Offerings and opening times vary year-round—check summertime possibilities of bundling your welllness day with a lunch menu at open-air restaurant Veranda.

• Atzaró Spa, Santa Eulària, atzaro.com

Barbecue Highway

The White Isle's finest red meat is to be found just off its dusty roads. *Cami de Balafia* (Sant Joan) is a hacienda with a magnificent courtyard like an orange grove. The secret to their grilled rabbit, beef and lamb is the combination of carob, olive and almond wood. Chips are hand-peeled by grandpa and the tomato salad is legendary. Prices aren't listed... But have faith in the quality. No reservations might mean a wait for the tree-sheltered garden at Santa Eulària's *Cas Pagés* (pictured)—preparing your appetite for gigantic portions. Aside from coal-grilled beef and wood-cooked lamb, "arroz matanza" is a soupy pork and chicken paella, and "sofrit pagès" is a spicy sausage stew. *Can Caus* (Santa Eulària) is a reconstruction of a traditional farmhouse and fulfils the same function with in-house cheese and embutido (cold cuts) production and a herd of goats. Try grilled sardines and barbecued goat with one of their local, organic wines. A former school became a node for local dishes in *Es Caliu* (Santa Eulària), with an antique waterwheel on the terrace and heroic lamb chops. It's open all year with a cosy fire in winter. Finally, the star of *Can Pilot* (Sant Antoni) is a kilo of t-bone ox steak finished at your table. The cool interior buzzes for lunch and the terrace is perfect for a star-gazing dinner. Book ahead.

• Various locations, see Index p. 63

Heather Harmon, Curator

Lost and Found

Heather Harmon
She moved from the US to Ibiza to open exhibitions spaces Art Projects Ibiza and Lune Rouge—and has received plenty of respect for her efforts. Her curatorial skills are precise, and her tendency to engage with locals during off-season shows a genuine bond with the community

Running galleries on Ibiza requires the constant hosting of artists and other visitors... meaning a curator is likely to become a psuedo tour guide before too long. Heather Harmon shares a breadth of Ibiza knowledge beyond the art world, recommending hikes among Roman aqueducts, phenomenal sunsets and salt-baked fish

How would you describe the island for those that have only heard the clichéd version? What's the year-round story?

It's an island of secrets and discoveries, whose population is an incredible mix of "locals" and international expats. Even the notion of being local is difficult to define—the island has been host to many cultures and settlers. When I first arrived, a friend told me that here people either "find or lose themselves," and this is true for many. The real secret is winter which is absolute paradise and doesn't resemble summer in any way. In this regard Ibiza is truly a tale of two cities, with winter and summer seasons paced in drastically different ways. For winter, the number of people on the island drops exponentially and you have an island almost to yourself with beautiful weather, climate and a magic all its own. For our exhibition spaces, we engage the local community at this time with lectures and events—inviting school groups, families and others invested in the future of Ibiza, as many businesses are seasonal and not open year-round. Staying open all year has introduced us to many who have loved and lived on the island for long periods of time.

You've been described as one of the "most powerful" people in the Ibizan art world. What's this art world like?

There are many histories in Ibiza, but the history of art, philosophy and architecture here is quite interesting. On this island you find artists, writers, curators, collectors, all gravitating here for their love of the place. From Walter Benjamin to Orson Welles, Ibiza has inspired many. The art community is thriving, free of the pace of a metropolitan city. People are engaged and this continues to grow

and change as our spaces create a place for people to connect.

Where should an art lover definitely go on the island?

Apart from my spaces, *Museu d'Art Contemporani* (MACE) is not to be missed. The museum's director Elena Ruiz Sastre is a pioneer and a force in Ibiza.

Are there any local artists you know of and whose work you admire?

Erwin Broner, architect and painter, is considered local and his Bauhaus-influenced canvases are steeped in the tradition of European abstract painting. His home and studio, Casa Broner, is marvelous, and also part of MACE.

What's your favourite way to get lost in Ibiza?

Hiking is amazing here. There's a long walk in Buscastell along the Roman aqueducts that is magical. The history of this island is fascinating and you can find yourself alone among Phoenician and Roman ruins all over the island. Also a must do is to catch a sunset—Ibiza has mind-blowing sunsets, some of the best I have ever seen.

What are some of the places you always take visiting friends?

To eat I like to stay local when possible, I love *Es Pins* for example, it's very traditional. There is a pop-up kitchen called *Ibiza Food Studio*, started by Boris Buono, that hosts some of the best and most inventive meals I have shared on the island. I always bring friends and visitors there. Another favourite is *Es Xarcu*. The people, food and view are among my favourites. A great place to find treasures is *Vicente Ganesha*, it's packed with vintage clothes. Also, *Pastis* in town is a French restaurant. It's great and open all year. The local owners are there every night. *Heart Ibiza* is incredible. It's an unparalleled fine dining and show experience, an amazing collaboration between the Adriá brothers and Cirque du Soleil. The food and performances are like no other.

What's your favourite beach/cala?
My favourite beach is *Sa Pedrera (Atlantis)*, which used to be a quarry. It is a hike to get there, but very much worth the effort.

Who makes the best paella?
I would recommend salt-baked fish over paella here. Paella originates in Valencia and Ibiza has a strong Mediterranean influence. Fish baked in salt is an Ibiza staple; there is a large salt deposit in Ses Salines. When a fresh-caught fish is baked in salt, it amplifies the moisture and makes for a delicacy. *El Chiringuito* is great for this dish. Other phenomenal local dishes are grilled calamari, sweet red shrimp, and gazpacho—the tomatoes in Ibiza are insanely good. Figs and almonds are wonderful here too. There is also a bakery called *La Canela* whose pastries are delicious.

What's the most inspiring spot on the island?
Es Vedrà. It is by far the most spectacular and special place on the island. It's a place of transformation—it is magnetic, powerful and stunningly beautiful.

Are there any locally produced things you always take to friends abroad?
There is a woman named Andrea who makes jams and spreads from local ingredients. She has a small stand on Saturdays at the *Forada Market* and Sundays at the *Sant Joan Market*. Her recipes

are a complex mix of flavours as she experiments and creates constantly. She's also a pleasure to talk with—I visit her often.

What does a perfect Formentera day look like?
Ferry over, rent a bicycle and head to *Beso Beach* for seafood.

Lots of people fantasise about dropping everything and moving to the island. How do you stay active in your trade while living there?
Ibiza is such a global hub so there are constant visitors keeping one active. In tandem, reading, travel and correspondence keeps me up on the art world. We always have artists, colleagues and clients in town. So one is never lonely here.

The legendary paella at restaurant Beso Beach alone is worth a trip to Formentera island

Transcendental Rock
Demystifying Es Vedrà

Javier Mendoza Cardona

Rising an imposing 382 metres above the waves in front of Ibiza's southeastern coast is Es Vedrà. This colossal pyramid pokes out of the Mediterranean thanks to some geological caprice. And thanks to a more human characteristic, a textured shroud of mystery surrounds the rock—one which continues to evolve even today.

Even as recently as early 2016, something happened to underline the kind of bizarre occurrences for years associated with Es Vedrà. More than 50 goats living there were slaughtered, the islet peppered with their abandoned carcasses.

Who was behind the massacre? A predator? Hunters on safari? No—the government of the Balearic Islands. Their aim was to protect the unique, native flora of the isle. Transporting the creatures alive was rejected, owing to the danger of the steep terrain. So the authorities decided to shoot the animals instead. And though they'd been introduced to the isle by man, many Ibizans went up in arms, and a demonstration protesting the slaughter coursed through the streets. Even high-ranking local clergyman Francesc Xavier Torres Peters got involved. He published proof that, even in 1315, herds of goats were already kept on Es Vedrà. The "Vedraners"—families who owned the isle—would hunt two or three goats every year for their own consumption. Custom prohibited carrying weapons on Es Vedrà, much less spilling blood, so the goats were corralled, tied up, and brought to Ibiza.

In the local press, opinions appeared citing the law of karma. If everything we do in life brings its consequences, the Ibizans should start to flee. The vengeance of the isle will surely be terrible.

Unravelling the Strings

We shouldn't be alarmed. for decades Es Vedrà has inspired a multitude of stories, myths and legends. Not long back in 2009 the Sant Joan local government published a press release featuring a supposed prophecy of noted soothsayer Nostradamus: "Ibiza will be the last refuge of the earth". In fact, Ibiza was never mentioned in any of Nostradamus's writings.

Popular culture has added to the texture of these myths. The long-told tale of the "The Giant of Es Vedrà" was put into writing by Joan Castelló i Guasch in 1953. It tells of a colossal inhabitant of the isle, who blocks passage to two brothers seeking a medicinal plant to cure their father.

The "Triangle of Silence" is a more recent myth. Echoing the Bermuda Triangle, there supposedly lies an area between the Mallorcan coast, Alicante's Penyal d'Ifac and Es Vedrà, where certain inexplicable events tend to happen. Birds become disorientated and navigational marine equipment goes haywire. The blame is put on Es Vedrà's magnetic influence. But though it's true compasses cannot function in some places of the earth, like Kursk in Russia and Bangui, Central African Republic—those two places boast a highly intense magnetic field. And none exists around Es Vedrà.

In 1950, Spanish newspaper "ABC" reported the conquest of Es

Vedrà's summit. Two Catalan mountain climbers were first to surmount its 382 metres. The article cited a local legend, that anyone who climbed Es Vedrà "would instantly change their sex." Though the men who did so clearly continued to be men—at least there were no reports to the contrary—the story shows such legends were around long before the arrival of mass tourism to Ibiza.

Naturally, extraterrestrials have also been dragged in. With a complete lack of photographic evidence, Es Vedrà's supposed magnetism has been related to a multitude of UFO sightings. And Unidentified Submerged Objects, or USOs, have also been reported. Divers have heard "mysterious" metallic noises, while fishermen have seen strange underwater lights beneath their boats. Perhaps coincidentally most sightings occurred during the 1970–1980s—the same time local hippy culture was flourishing.

Writer and investigator Josep Riera claimed that Es Vedrà is a stone watchtower that protects the island of Ibiza. And Mariano Planells, in his "Dictionary of the Secrets of Ibiza" (1982), argued that the isle is a gigantic energy accumulator employed by aliens. Even today many of the tourists who view the sunset from that side will claim that the rock recharges their energy.

It's no wonder Es Vedrà has been converted into an icon. Musician Mike Oldfield photographed himself with the rock in the background for his "Tubular Bells III" album cover. And the most famous brand of traditional local liquor hierbas ibicencas carries the isle's image on its bottles.

Blurred Lines

For the creation of a legend it's necessary to blur the lines between myth and fact. Not everything said about Es Vedrà is simple fantasy. The isle has a singular beauty, and it's been the protagonist of some fascinating stories that have served to boost its fame.

Possibly the seed of all these legends was sown by Catalan Carmelite Francisco Palau who, for political reasons, was forced into exile on Ibiza in the mid-19th century. He decided to realise various spiritual retreats on Es Vedrà. According to existing documentation he was the first inhabitant of the isle—and, certainly, he is the person who has spent the most time living there. The rock offered him shelter in a small cave furnished with a trickle of freshwater to drink. And other essentials were provided periodically by vessels that passed by.

In "Francisco Palau and Ibiza" various of his impressions of the isle are included from the letters he wrote at the time, such as:

"Having retired to this mountain, a great 20-year-old voice spoke to me in the deserts about the destiny of our Order; I did not know from whence it came."

Voices on a desert isle? Many have related the experiences of Father Palau with mystical meetings, perhaps of alien origin. But it's doubtless that prolonged isolation on an isle with such extreme conditions could have unexpected consequences.

Nevertheless, Father Palau should not be totally discredited, since his memory has been kept alive on Ibiza. He's considered the founder of Es Cubells, where he built the chapel upon which the village's church was later constructed. A bust of the hermit stands next to it today. And on its pedestal is engraved the silhouette of a certain mystical rock: recalling the great influence Es Vedrà had upon him.

Another key event happened a few decades back, on November 11, 1979. Close to midnight, an aeroplane with 109 passengers was flying from Palma de Mallorca to Tenerife. Just southeast of Ibiza—close to Es Vedrà—the pilot, Captain Lerdo de Tejada observed two fixed red lights just three miles from the plane.

Contrasted with other such cases, that night's events are amply documented. In conversations with the control centres of Madrid and Barcelona, the pilot's voice betrays increasing anxiety. He asks what other vessels could be occupying that aerial space—while relaying that the two red lights are getting closer. They are now within just half a mile of the plane. The controllers insist that nothing could possibly be flying in the zone. Responding to the pilot's desperation, they finally make an unheard-of decision: to divert the plane to land at the airport of Manises in Valencia. Spanish aviation history had its first-ever forced landing by UFO.

The media called it the "Manises Case"—it had everything for journalists to fill hundreds of pages. The Spanish army embarked on a hunt the next day, combing the area from every direction. The Spanish parliament even spoke about the case. And still today no definitive explanation has been made. The best speculation is that the night's excellent visibility enabled the reflection of factory chimneys on the Spanish coast to be seen in the water.

Es Vedrà guards many more secrets: a small lighthouse invisible from Ibiza, a large cross on the summit placed by a clergyman more than 50 years ago, and a subspecies of green-blue lizard found nowhere else in the world. Fortunately, visits are prohibited without special permission. This is nothing to do with the isle's status as the private property of various Ibizan families. Instead, it belongs to a Natural Reserve to preserve its flora and fauna— bringing us back to the vanquished goats.

And it's better to keep it protected. Some places should remain wrapped in their mysteries.

Javier Mendoza Cardona was born in 1985 in Ibiza. A rabid history and culture buff, he's also passionate about hiking, running, photography and comics. Since 2009 his online guide ibizaisla.es has covered some of the stranger sides of the island

Sid Shanti, Chef

Kitchen Days

<u>Sid Shanti</u>
He has performed as private chef on the island for VIPs like Puff Daddy, Jade Jagger—and even fellow cuisinier Jamie Oliver. The Brit is also the author of "Glorious Ibiza Food (& Music!)", a cookbook containing not only his favourite summer recipes but also tips for local suppliers. Sid organises private dinner packages, a summer pop-up restaurant, and even an annual event in October, Shantico, where he cooks up some tunes from behind the decks

After almost two decades Sid still enjoys the diversity and tolerance ingrained into the DNA of Ibiza. As a chef and passionate cook, he shares his insights on the markets and dining scene. As a connoisseur he prefers the joy of simple, traditional food. Contain your hunger while reading, as Sid takes us on a culinary island trip

When did you come to Ibiza and what did you do before?

I first came to the island in 1998. At the time I was a touring DJ in the psychedelic trance movement. "Manumission", a very well known party at the time on Ibiza, brought me here to play for them at the club Privilege. Previously, I had been a chef for many years and had completed my studies in classical French cuisine and gained a wide knowledge of kitchens through my apprenticeship at the Groucho Club in London, as well as working at many other establishments. I took time out from cooking professionally from around 1994 when my DJ commitments became full time and touring became my full-time profession.

The island's changed its face very fast since then...

It's true that the island has changed dramatically over the last decade or so. But that said, everywhere changes with time, right? Some aspects have remained true to form: you can still eat in local restaurants that capture the original sentiment of the island, find secluded beaches with crystal clear water—and equally you can still find parties that are rich in spirit and attended by many like-minded people. The clubbing scene is still vibrant and easily holds its position in the world. Currently though, Ibiza is experiencing a change in its gastronomic offering, with many chefs from around the world wanting a platform here for their skills. This is reflected in new offerings at beach clubs, night-time cabaret restaurants and providers of bespoke products that chefs and restaurateurs might struggle to find in the most cosmopolitan of cities.

Talking about new chefs from all over the world that come here—which of those new fine dining occasions are worth experiencing?

Well it is hard to define what is worth the cost. To one person a dinner for a thousand euros may provide an extremely enjoyable evening, to another a simple "menu del dia" for ten euros will suffice—with both parties leaving and feeling fulfilled on many levels. Beauty and value are in the eye of the beholder. I'd recommend experiencing the cabaret at *Lio*, owned and run by Pacha, and also *Heart*, owned and run by Guy Laliberté and Ferran Adrià. Both are expensive but truly entertaining. For atmosphere I'd dine at *Bambuddha Grove*. For food I prefer local and simple. The grilled squid and local chips at *Es Canto* in Santa Gertrudis are to die for!

Where else can the traditional and original flavours of the island be experienced?

Can Caus on the road to Santa Gertrudis for instance offers local lamb, goat and suckling pig, and is authentic to the core. Simple grilled meats. The walls are adorned with scores of old black and white photos of Ibizan times gone by. For incredibly delicious toasted breads with Pata Negra ham or cured sheep's cheese go to *Bar Costa* in Santa Gertrudis. The quality of this simple offering is the highest and the walls of the restaurant—be sure to walk all the way through, it's huge—are covered with one of the biggest private collections of surrealist art in Spain. These paintings were traded for food and drink by some of the many artists that lived on Ibiza during the 1960s and 1970s. Another firm favourite is *Cami de Balafia* on the road to Sant Joan, a classic Spanish grill serving vegetables from their land and meat that has been reared with love. It has a charming terrace with small fruit trees and bougainvillea flowers aplenty. And *KM 5* is a very good restaurant—the owner Josh is an Ibiza veteran. The restaurant has undergone many improvements over the years but still holds an Ibiza magic and the kitchen serves very good food.

Which dish shouldn't be missed?
"Bullit de peix", a classic Ibizan fish stew with potatoes and local fish, rich in flavour and colour. The best place to eat this is on a sunny afternoon is on the terrace at restaurant *Es Boldado* in Cala d'Hort. The views of Es Vedrà are second to none from this restaurant. Or try restaurant *Es Xarcu* just past the bay of Cala Jondal. This place has a beautiful rustic charm— it's on the ocean and serves great fish dishes.

Is there really still fish in the ocean here or does it all come by plane?
The oceans around Ibiza certainly don't have as many fish as many years ago. That said it is still possible to fish and catch them. It would be impossible and unethical for restaurants on the island to only serve wild fish given the numbers of people that visit Ibiza each year. Most restaurants serve fish from sustainable sources, like fish farms in the Mediterranean. But most good fish restaurants have wild offerings on the menu—you just need to ask. *Restaurante Sa Caleta* serves very good wild fish as do most of the others mentioned above. I tend to order John Dory, in Spanish "Gallo San Pedro", this fish is always wild and sold in all fish restaurants, baked in the oven. Whole.

If I rent a finca for my stay... Where could I get fresh, organic ingredients for some home cooking?
There are many markets on Ibiza and depending on where you stay will denote where you should buy from. In the north, *Es Mercat* in Santa Eulària is a very good local market selling fish, meat and vegetables. Also in Ibiza Town, the *Mercat Nou* has the same offering. Many organic farms sell direct to customers as well. The best way to find out who and when they open is to look online: *Can Pere Mussona, Can Muson, Ca Na Berri, Sa Posta* and *Sa Bassa Roja.*

Is there also good wine from the island?
The northern area surrounding Sant Mateu is the main wine-growing region. The wines produced here range from delicious blush rosé— look for Ibizkus—to reds that would be better used as a vinegar for salad dressing! Another wine producer, Can Rich, have an organic vineyard near to Sant Antoni, and they have a range of decent wines available in most shops on the island. They also produce olive oil and very good herbs.

As a chef, do you also cook at home —and if so, what?
Sure! I love to cook! I cook roast Sunday lunches with "Pollo Payes"—locally reared chicken and an array of vegetables direct from the farms I use to supply my catering business. I do a barbeque with lamb from the island and infuse the fire with wild rosemary picked in the forest, served with salad from my garden... Or I make a paella for friends with fish from the waters close to the island. I also like lazy days in the kitchen at home where I'll make a tuna spaghetti bolognese or a simple soup.

Sid's private dinner includes fishing for your own produce, watching the sunset, then dining in a candlelit cove

What is the music you prefer to listen to while cooking?

I like to listen to the music mixes of Ibiza DJs Jon Sa Trinxa, Andy Wilson, Alfredo, Graham Sahara and Howard Hill. Great Balearic summer music.

Talking about the future. What are your wishes for Ibiza in the year 2025?

That the island continues to keep its inherent values of patience, tolerance, acceptance and respect. That it remains the number-one destination for attracting free thinkers, thrill seekers, beach bums and movie stars, models and hippies, royalty and poverty, techno kids and house heads, alternative minds and intelligent souls. That the offerings and infrastructure continue to improve and diversify... And above all that the waters of the ocean remain free of pollution and the sun beats down day by day on the beautiful land and virgin coastline.

Muses and Mascots

Curated by Armin Heinemann

Paula's opened doors in 1972, quickly transcending its status as clothing boutique to become a cultural powerhouse. Behind it was tireless and prolific Armin Heinemann, local legend and current head of the Ibiza Opera Festival. Though the shop is but a memory, these extracts from the book "Paula's Ibiza 25 Años" bear witness to that era of free-wheeling, free-spirited madness

Rossetta Montenegro, Publicist

Island Legend

Back in 1972 when Rossetta started at Pacha, it was just a tiny
house in the countryside. Things have changed since then, though
her love for the job and the island have only grown stronger.
Here she shares her secrets including spots for cycling incognito
and a beachside sardine feast

Many clubs don't make it past the first couple of years—how has Pacha made it to 43?

I think part of the secret is in that the building where Pacha is housed has a uniquely spectacular energy. There isn't a DJ that doesn't love to play there, because it sounds perfect. You can be on the dancefloor with the music blasting, but you can still have a conversation with someone. It's always been like that, the room was made perfectly. Pacha is also a way of life. Every time you walk in you know you'll run into someone who knows you. It's like a big family, and that's always evident. Every person who works there—and there are 700 of us—feels love for the group and puts a little of themselves into it. I love Pacha, it's such a big part of my life. If I see a piece of litter on the floor, I pick it up. It's a temple of fun we all take care of and put our love into. And I think that shows. We have a very special type of audience, and they find each other here. I think that's the secret. It also helps that we've known how to market the franchise all over the world—the cherries have made their way across the globe.

What's your first memory of Ibiza?

It was 1972, I first arrived here and immediately realised it was paradise. The spectacular beaches were empty at that time and the air smelled of rosemary and Mediterranean hierbas. I remember that very clearly. Those years were marvellous; there were very few people in Ibiza and it was all very free.

And your first party?

I was at the inauguration of Pacha in 1973. It was in a tiny house and all our friends were there, including the owner of the club. By day we'd all go to

Formentera and every night we'd come back to Pacha. Sometimes we'd even show up in our bathing suits, sarong and all. It wasn't like now where people really dress up to go to the disco. It was more relaxed. We also liked to wear costumes, so we'd have themed nights and, say, on African night, we'd come as lions or in tribal paint. There was always a reason to celebrate and get into character.

What was the neighbourhood like in those days?

Pacha was a little house in the countryside and people would tell us "I'll never go there, it's so far". These days it's right in the middle of the centre—it's become an integral part of the city. At that time the hippy movement was at its prime. People would come from everywhere and nobody cared about the day, the hour or their phones. To talk to my mother I'd have to go to an operator in the Hotel Montesol, who would work the switchboard and direct me to a cabin. So of course we'd only speak to our parents once every two weeks.

What's your favourite way to get lost in Ibiza?

I love to get lost in Formentera —I rent a bike and go completely unnoticed. I always go through San Francisco (Sant Francesc), buy a sandwich and see the shops. Any deli or market will make you a good sandwich, though I must say the best is at *Can Pep Tixedó* supermarket on the road into Ses Salines. In Formentera there's a little shop where an Italian lady knits woollen fishermen's sweaters —right on the strip in Sant Francesc.

In four decades of leading the world's club scene, Pacha has kept its electric personality alive

What's your favourite place to have a caña and watch people go by?

Well, I've never had a beer in my life, but I can tell you my favourite place to have natural juices is *Es Tap Nou* in Ibiza centre. They have a juice of the day every day. I also love *Canadian*, they make a great apple-ginger-carrot juice. There's a big cult of health in Ibiza so there's many places to have a good juice. In the Marina there's a café called *Cappuccino* where you can sit and have your juice with a view of Dalt Vila, while you watch some of the most spectacular yachts come into the port.

Where to have dinner when there's something to celebrate?

The *Pacha* restaurant does a spectacular fusion of Mediterranean-Japanese cuisine. I eat there almost every Saturday, the black cod is to die for.

Is there any place that's been around forever you still like to go to?

There's a place in Santa Agnès called *Can Cosmi*. They make a spectacular potato tortilla, and it's been there for a lifetime. It's basically the only attraction in the town besides the church and the cemetery, and we love to go there in February to see the almond trees in bloom. There are about 4,000 trees that blossom at the same time. It's paradise, with the smell of the trees and the flowers. In Can Cosmi they make chocolate cake, tortilla and salad—not much else.

Also, right next to the port of Sant Miquel there's a place on Caló des Multons beach called *Utopía* where they grill sardines on sticks. Every Friday, for 15 euros, you can eat all the sardines you want. There's also *Can Pau*, which has been open for 45 years, with good reason.

Favourite beach for when you don't want anyone to find you?

If I want to disappear, I go up to Sant Miquel, leave my car and hike for about an hour. After you hike up a hill, you find a tiny cove at the bottom called *Es Portitxol*. Right now that's impossible for me because I have no time, so I go to *Es Cavallet*, which I love off season without the umbrellas and the chairs.

Who makes the best paella?

The best fideuá and paella is at *Can Salinas Manuel*. *La Escollera* in Es Cavallet is also good. Paella and fideuá are typical Spanish dishes; they seem like they're very easy to make but it's not that simple to get them perfect. Sometimes people put too much oil, they burn the rice or the noodles are too soft. It's a classic Sunday dish in every home but not every restaurant does it well.

Where do you go to buy something special?

I love to go to *Las Dalias* market, I honestly believe it's the best market in the entire world—and I've been around the world. You have the hippies from the 1970s who are still around, dressed exactly the same as always, but they're 80 years old now. They still go and sell their things and travel to markets all around the world. You can find everything there, things from Pakistan, India, Afghanistan, Uruguay. It's very interesting.

Are there any spots on the island that take your breath away?

Sa Caleta is a site that dates back to 6 BC, a Phoenician settlement right across from Es Vedrá that is supposed to be sacred. There's a very special energy there, which is I think why the Phoenicians chose it. You can see the ruins, they're very well conserved—where they lived, where they stored their oil, their water tank. It's a special place to watch the sun set. Near this spot there's an Ibizan restaurant called *Es Boldado*, they make bullit payés, which is a fish stew typical of the island. It's made from Ibizan potato, fish and rice. They cook it all together but then they serve the broth first, then the fish and then the potatoes.

Take local fish stew "bullit payés" at Es Boldado and gaze, the other way, at Es Vedrà

Eivissa

City of Riches

Drag queens on stilts bounding down ancient alleys while grandma cooks up a Spanish storm... Eivissa is many things, including the nerve centre of a sleepy island that washes away its sins with every sunrise over the fortress walls

Culture | **Dawn of Creation**

In the 1960s, Ibiza pulled artists in like a magnet. The promise of positive vibes, sunshine, semi-seclusion and creative openness was irresistible. And this story of artistic creation on the island is documented in style at *Museu d'Art Contemporani*. The iconic building holds renaissance murals and even a weapons room. And below the building, architectural remnants of the 6th century Phoenician settlement can be seen. Also part of the museum is Casa Broner—the modernist Sa Penya apartment and studio of German-Jewish architect and painter Erwin Bronner—now restored and opened to the public. Broner fled

the Nazis to Ibiza in 1934. He was a founding member of avant-garde collective Grupo Ibiza 59 and designed some 50 buildings on the island— his work becoming a pivotal influence. Check the museum's programme—recent activities include breakfasts in collaboration with neighbouring art space Lune Rouge. The gallery directors drink coffee along with attendees, encouraging a relaxed exchange and an inspiring start to another creative day on Ibiza.
• Museu d'Art Contemporani, Ronda Narcis Putget, Eivissa, eivissa.es/mace

Heads Up

In Ibiza, a good hat is practically a birthright. And *Sombrería Bonet* has been a trusted source of shade for island residents for more than 100 years of business—making it one of the two oldest operating stores in the area. Open since 1916, the hat-maker is still in the hands of the same family—who have embraced the 21st century with an enthusiastic use of Facebook, while continuing to specialise in classic shapes and quality fabrications. From Panama to Pamela, Bonet has it covered. Your head, that is.
• Sombrería Bonet, Calle Comte de Rossello 6, Eivissa

Food **Simple Delights**

The big spenders, the jet set, the glitz and glamour —you won't find any of that among the surviving old-school restaurants that still make Ibiza what it is. *Comida Bar San Juan* is an unpretentious institution of a restaurant popular with locals on their lunch breaks, next to whom you just might be seated at one of the tables. Down the street is *Can Gourmet*, a tiny hole in the wall slinging some of the best bocadillos in town, with a few local delicacies available to take back home.
• Eivissa, various locations, see Index p. 63

Night **Dance like a Local**

Yes, it's possible to go clubbing in Ibiza town without spending a fortune on entry fees and drinks. *Veto Social Club* might be neighboured to the glamorous Pacha—but the concept is almost the opposite. The electronic music program is not built around big names; instead of multiple VIP areas you'll find a raw, almost industrial ambiance. The only fancy décor is the collection of car lamps behind the DJ booth.
• Veto Social Club, Avinguda 8 d'Agost, 7–11, Eivissa, veto-social-club.com

Old City Cocktails

A world away from the din of the centre, there are few things as romantic as wandering the tiny labyrinthine alleys of D'alt Vila. A perfect way to punctuate your promenade is with a drink and bite on one of the hidden terraces in the village. A fine candidate is *Bar 1805*, which dishes out French-style comfort food and a slick selection of cocktails—all created by owner and mixmaster Charles. Come for the moules frites, stay for the French absinthe drip.

• Bar 1805, Calle Santa Llùcia 7, Eivissa, bar1805ibiza.com

Food **French Letter**

Just off the delightfully busy Plaza del Parque in Eivissa centre is a tiny, unassuming restaurant you might just walk past were it not for the eager recommendations of longtime patrons. For French cuisine with a Mediterranean flair, this island brasserie is, expectedly, not a budget-minded option. But it's narrow, elegant interior with the kitchen on display, plus finely prepared dishes like the steak tartare, make it a good reward after a hard day splashing in the sea.

• Restaurante Pastis, Calle Avicenna 2, Eivissa, pastisibiza.com

Night **Hop this Way**

Colourful Calle de la Virgen in the middle of old Ibiza town might just be one of the last true expressions of authentic Ibizan nocturnal culture left on the island. From drag queens on stilts to endless parades of sculpted men promoting parties, this is one of the best streets in town for barhopping and people watching. And a mandatory stop on any crawl should be *Bar Leon*, a small, eccentric watering hole run by Erwin, whose collection of stuffed toy lions and other knick-knacks presides over the bottles.

• Bar Leon, Calle de la Virgen 62, Eivissa, bar-leon.de

Treasure Island

Ibiza may be much more than endless nights and glamour, but if you're going to do it, you might as well look the part. Enter *Le Studio*, a veritable treasure trove of a boutique in old Eivissa. The shop was born when Fanny and Annie, two former party promoters with serious style chops, decided to drop everything and set up shop. Luxe vintage gems flown in from around the world hang beside custom creations in an explosion of sequins, florals, silk and tulle perfect for channeling your inner Studio 54 diva.
• Le Studio, Carrer de Manuel Sorà 17, Eivissa, lestudioibiza.com

Night | **Nocturnal Jammin'**

Having offered a stage for live music since 1988, *Teatro Pereyra* is a classic. And it remains a solid pillar of the capital's nightlife, with a blend of locals and tourists. The target group is 30-plus and the music reflects the taste: from 11pm on bands rock the old theatre—mostly with a programme at the intersection of jazz, rock and soul. The musicians are top drawer and even if most songs are covers—their jamming talent always fills the dancefloor. Start out with cheaper drinks on the terrace.
• Teatro Pereyra, Calle del Conde de Rosselló, 3, Eivissa, teatropereyra.combar1805ibiza.com

Food | **Tapas Time**

Under the Old City walls, *La Bodega* is an Ibizan mainstay: persevere for an outside table—though the interior has a cluttered charm—and stay all night. Pulpo, gambas or provolone cheese match with excellent Rioja, and the staff gushes with charisma. Downtown, *Can Terra* is a sophisticated venue for tapas, or "pintxo" to be exact, as the snacks are served on bread (pictured). Stand by the bar to seize the morsels directly, or sit in the elegant courtyard. Next door *El Zaguan* is a quintessential, well-priced tapas bar, whose quality is proven by the presence of local families.
• Eivissa, various locations, see Index p.63

Sabrina Serrat & Tom Preuss, Fashion Designer & Promoter

Well Seasoned

Sabrina Serrat & Tom Preuss
She is originally from Barcelona
and works as a fashion designer
and creative director. He grew
up in Dusseldorf, Germany, and
promotes the event series HYTE,
while also running the Berlin
based booking agency Artist
Alife. Both are proud residents
of the White Isle where
they are, in addition to all that,
also parents

Ibiza's proximity to the rest of Europe has turned it into the ideal headquarters for Tom and Sabrina. And though club culture is an integral part of their life, the couple sheds light on what else island life has to offer both on- and off-season—including molecular dining and an excursion to a hidden cove

Some people have those "a-ha" moments before big life changes—did you have an Ibiza epiphany that made you realise you had to be here?

Tom: I came to Ibiza for the first time as a boy 18 years ago and fell in love with the island. It motivated me to do what I do today and inspired every single party and event I ever did—I wanted every experience to be as good as when I experienced the Sunday terrace at Space for the first time. In that sense it's always been a huge part of my life. All the artists I've managed and worked with have created some of their most defining moments here, and everything in my career has been connected to the island in some way or another.

Sabrina: I just love the rhythm of the island. Everything flows here and time doesn't really exist. It's a melting pot of interesting people from all over the world, you are two hours away from any big city in Europe, the sun shines pretty much all year round and you are surrounded by water which gives you a sense of space and freedom. It's a bit special.

You live here with your young son. Which particular restaurants, beaches, parties or activities are best enjoyed with the family?

Sabrina: We love big lunches at *El Chiringuito* in Platja d'Es Cavallet with friends and family or a nice day out on a boat to Formentera. In general Ibiza is a great place for families—everywhere is really family friendly, with kids, a dog—you can do everything together.

Of course the beaches are a big pull, do you have hidden gems you'd share?

Tom: We like to go to *Cala Pluma*, in between Ses Salines beach and Es Cavallet. If you go there early season or at the end of it you can get your own private beach. It's paradise. But high season is a completely different story. In the winter, *Platja d'en Bossa* is also incredible—two kilometres of beautiful, clear waters and white sand. But in the peak season it's hell on earth!

You're both lovers of good food. What are your tips for creative dining?

Sabrina: For creative dining I'd say *Heart*. It's the restaurant from Ferran Adriá who is one of the most amazing chefs in the world and Guy Laliberté, the founder of Cirque du Soleil. I think that says it all.

Tom: During the season, Heart definitely leads the way with creative dining. Ferran Adriá is known for his molecular gastronomy, and the combination with Guy's vision is super creative. Also, the street-food terrace with international flavours that they have is something unique on the island.

And if I wanted some the authentic old-school food, where would you take me?

Tom: It's no longer an island secret, but *Cami de Balafia* is without doubt the best restaurant for authentic food. It's run by an Ibizan family. The menu is so simple but they have the best meat, delicious tomato salads, and the setting is unbeatable—a charming garden where you sit under a giant tree. We have vegan friends who eat meat once a year only at Balafia—it's that good.

Sabrina: Another favourite is *Comida Bar San Juan* in Ibiza Town, a super local place only open for a couple of hours for lunch and dinner. There's no reservations and if you're not there at opening time you don't get a table. Those in the know ask for the special menu which they don't offer up—it has a couple of dishes each day which are strictly for locals.

Not everyone wants to party with thousands of others... Tom, as a promoter, could you recommend any alternative to the megaclubs?

Tom: Honestly if you really come to party in Ibiza you will often end up going to one of the mega-clubs. You really cannot find that intensity and atmosphere anywhere else around the world. But if they're really not for you then it's all about the after-parties and villa parties in the hills. The off-season is a different story again though, and *Pacha* always has a great selection of music throughout the winter. We've been throwing our monthly "People Like Us" parties there and the vibe has been great—using the smaller room, with an open fire in the middle of the club makes for a really cosy atmosphere. Also the "Keep On Dancing" parties on Sundays at *Lips* are where everybody comes together during the winter.

Sabrina, the fashion scene has changed in Ibiza. What are the latest shops and designers not to miss?

Sabrina: Vali! This is a new label from the island owned by dear friends of mine who grew up here. Their clothes are the perfect embodiment of Ibiza cool.

If you have a babysitter—what's your favourite way to get lost in Ibiza?

Sabrina: I rarely go out anymore but if I do, I prefer villa parties over clubs, or venues which are open-air areas like *DC10* or *Beachouse*, which is right on the beach.

How and where do you nurse a nasty hangover?

Sabrina: A healthy stop at *Passion* for some nice fresh juices and good food and a swim at the beach to wash your sins away.

Tom: I really enjoy spending a day at one of the beach clubs—even the commercial ones can be really nice. Hanging out at *Tropicana* in Cala Jundal is a great way to spend the day recovering.

What could any European capital learn from Ibiza?

Sabrina: There's a certain mindset that sets people apart and creates a really unique vibe here. It's an alternative way of caring about your life and being more aware.

Tom: It's about being open-minded and appreciating things out of the mainstream. That's something which a lot of other cities lack.

And, conversely, what is Ibiza lacking to be the perfect place to live in?

Tom: I couldn't watch "Star Wars" in 3D here, so a big cinema! Especially for the winter time. And in in the summer an open-air cinema. I even set up my own once, but the wind blew the screen away. So there's definitely a gap in the market for that!

Some days an open-air groove beats a megaclub… At Beachouse, for example

Under the Sun

Sun Screen

Born in Ibiza, this line of handmade sunglasses shows serious some island love with models named after Portinatx and Atlantis.
• Atlantis sunglasses, Capote Eyewear, capoteyewear.com

Carrying On

Picking up a "capazo", or hand-woven basket is one way to bring the island vibes back home, but the charm of the summer accessory fades as temperatures drop. Enter the winter version: cosy, wool-covered and waiting for you at the little shack in Es Cavallet's parking lot.
• Winter capazo

Look Book

Pick up a piece of Ibiza history by way of this luxurious tome, weighing in at about three kilos and featuring what must be the finest documentation of 1970–80s island madness. Each limited-edition copy, printed in 1997, is stamped and numbered. See some stunning extracts in our photo showcase.
• "Paula's Ibiza 25 Años", Libreria Vara de Rey, Eivissa, libreriavaraderey.com

Books

Experience and Poverty
• Walter Benjamin, 1933

Philosopher Walter Benjamin was another one drawn to the freedom of Ibiza. Following a friend from the horrors of Nazi Berlin to the isle's sunnier shores, he drafted there one of his lesser-known essays. The master in the art of getting lost walked extensively on the White Isle as he developed his arguments about the dangers of modernity and the importance of narrative.

Life and Death of a Spanish Town
• Elliot Paul, 1937

US author Elliot Paul, friend to Stein and Joyce in the heady times of 1930s Paris, fled to Ibiza after a nervous breakdown, only for the Spanish Civil War to break out. His book tells of a serene society ripped apart by conflict, and proved so controversial to the authorities that it was only published in Spanish in 2005.

Tal and the Magic Barruget
• Eva-Lis Wuorio, 1965

During a summer spent in an Ibizan village eight-year-old Tal is distracted from his father's new marriage by witchy housekeeper Bruja Vieja—who summons a goblin, or barruget, to liven things up. A colourful classic for kids.

Films

More
• Barbet Schroeder, 1969

The sun-drenched precursor to "Trainspotting" tells the tale of fast youth and young death at the crossroads of freedom and excess. The film bursts with iconic shots of the White Isle, and marked a turning point for soundtrack producers Pink Floyd.

F For Fake
• Orson Welles, 1974

The maestro of cinematic trickery turned to another famous fraudster in his last major work: art forger Elmyr de Hory, who spent years hiding on Ibiza. Welles reflects on the nature of hoax in the form-busting documentary.

It's All Gone Pete Tong
• Michael Dowse, 2004

Ibizan DJ Frankie Wilde goes too deep into the scene—and comes out deaf, wifeless and friendless... Told with cameos from stars Carl Cox, Paul Van Dyk and even Tong himself, this mockumentary captures the clichés and reality of Ibiza club culture and DJ worship.

Music

Sketches from an Island
• Marc Barrott, 2015

Polyrhythmic beats, birdsong, flute—but nothing kitschy in this new Balearic classic. International Feel's Marc Barrott takes from Cluster, Brian Eno and Tangerine Dream, blending it like a master. For a hot afternoon in the campo.

Technique
• New Order, 1989

Put off producing yet another album in dark, grey London, New Order relocated to Ibiza in 1988. The result was one of their most convincing front-to-back efforts. Influenced by Acid House, the sun and Balearic beats, "Technique" marked New Order's final departure from being a rock band.

Various DJ Sets
• Alfredo, DJ Pippi, etc.

Ibiza Airport fills up in summer with gold-digger DJs' private jets. But don't forget forerunners like Alfredo and Pippi who've shaped the island's sound since the 1980s. They're the real stars behind the Balearic decks.
• soundcloud.com/lost-in-the-city/sets/ibiza

LOST iN

The City

Getting lost in the city is not about throwing away the map
It's about surrendering yourself to the essence of the place
The art and creativity that provide its individual inspiration
The sights, smells, flavours and sounds that make it unique

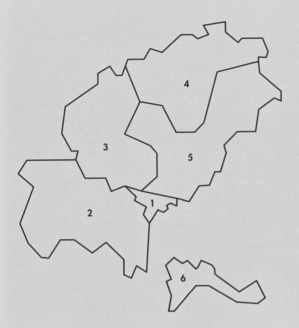

Districts

1 / Eivissa

2/Sant Josep

Atlantis (Sa Pedrera de Cala d'Hort)
Torrent d'en
Pere Massa
→ p. 15 Ⓞ

**Bar Restaurant
Es Cubells**
Carrer es Cubells 2, 1,
Es Cubells
→ p. 16 Ⓕ

Beachouse
Carretera de Platja
d'en Bossa, 2, Sant
Jordi de ses Salines
+34 971 39 68 58
beachouseibiza.com
→ p. 58 Ⓕ

Ca na Berri
Camí de Cas Colls
+34 651 13 51 93
canaberri.blogspot.
com → p. 32 Ⓢ

Cala Bassa (beach)
+34 902 30 04 44
Carretera de Cala
Conta → p. 15 Ⓞ

Cala Comte (beach)
Carretera de
Cala Conta
+34 971 80 01 25
→ p. 15 Ⓞ

Cala Pluma (beach)
Carrer la Canal–2
→ p. 57 Ⓞ

Can Salinas Manuel
Carretera de Salinas,
km 3.7 → p. 50 Ⓕ

DC10
Carretera PM-802
+44 7956 277484
→ p. 58 Ⓝ

El Chiringuito de María
Cap Martinet
→ p. 11 Ⓕ

**El Chiringuito
Es Cavallet**
Platja des Cavallet
+34 971 39 54 85
→ p. 24, 57 Ⓕ

Es Cavallet (beach)
Cami de Cavallet
→ p. 50 Ⓞ

Es Xarcu
Cala Es Xarco
+34 971 18 78 67
esxarcu.com
→ p. 23, 32 Ⓕ

Km 5
Carretera Sant Josep
km 5
+34 971 39 63 49
km5-lounge.com
→ p. 20, 22 Ⓕ

La Escollera
Platja des Cavallet
+34 971 39 65 72
laescolleraibiza.com
→ p. 50 Ⓕ

Platja d'en Bossa
(beach)
Carretera Platja d'en
Bossa
+34 971 30 19 59
→ p. 57 Ⓞ

Restaurant Es Torrent
Platja d'es Torrent
+34 971 80 21 60
estorrent.net
→ p. 11 Ⓕ

**Restaurante Es
Boldado**
Camí de Cala d'Hort
+34 626 49 45 37
restaurante
boldado.net
→ p. 32, 50 Ⓕ

Restaurante Sa Caleta
Platja d'es Bol Nou
+34 971 18 70 95
restaurante
sacaleta.com
→ p. 16, 32 Ⓕ

Sant Agustí des Vedrà
(village)
→ p. 14 Ⓞ

Super Ca'n Pep Tixedó
Camí de la Revista,
Sant Francesc
de s'Estany
supercanpeptixedo.
com → p. 48 Ⓢ

Tropicana Beach Club
Cala Jundal
+34 971 18 75 20
tropicanaibiza.com
→ p. 58 Ⓕ

3/Sant Antoni

Cala Salada (beach)
Camí Cala Salada
→ p. 10 Ⓞ

Can Cosmi
Plaça de l'Església,
Santa Agnès de
Corona
+34 971 80 50 20
→ p. 16, 49 Ⓕ

Can Pilot
Carretera Eivissa-Sant
Antoni, Sant Rafel
+34 971 19 82 93
asadorcanpilot.com
→ p. 10 Ⓕ

Es Broll (valley)
→ p. 15 Ⓞ

Forada Market
Carretera Santa Agnès
km 5, Forada
+34 971 34 52 48
→ p. 24 Ⓢ

Punta Galera
Carrer Número 2
Punta Galera, 6
→ p. 10 Ⓞ

Sa Bassa Roja
Carretera Santa
Agnès, km 3.4
+34 659 37 86 65
sabassaroja.es
→ p. 31 Ⓢ

**Santa Agnès de
Corona** (village)
→ p. 14 Ⓞ

The Lost City
Cala d'Albarca
→ p. 14 Ⓞ

Underground Ibiza
Diseminado Cas
Arabins, 96
Sant Rafel
+34 971 19 86 56
→ p. 10 Ⓝ

4/Sant Joan

Aguas Blancas (beach)
Carrer Punta Grossa
→ p. 10 Ⓞ

Cala Xuclar (beach)
Carretera San Joan–
Portinatx, km 26.5
→ p. 10 Ⓞ

Camí de Balafia
Lugar Venda de
Balafia de Dalt, 25
+34 971 32 50 23
→ p. 21, 31, 57 Ⓕ

Can Curune
Carretera a Port de
Sant Miquel
→ p. 16 Ⓕ

Chiringuito Utopia
Caló des Moltons
→ p. 50 Ⓕ

Es Pins
Carretera C-733, km
14.8
+34 971 32 50 34
→ p. 23 Ⓕ

Es Portitxol (beach)
→ p. 15, 50 Ⓞ

Estanco Can Xicu
Carrer de Missa, 7,
Sant Miquel
→ p. 19 Ⓝ

Restaurante la Paloma
Carrer Can Pou, 4,
Sant Llorenç
+34 971 32 55 43
palomaibiza.com
→ p. 19 Ⓕ

S'illot des Rencli
Lugar Venda Niu
Corps, 26
→ p. 16 Ⓕ

Sant Joan Market
Plaza de España, Sant
Joan de Labritja
→ p. 20, 24 Ⓢ

The Giri Café
Calle Principal, 5
Sant Joan de Labritja
+34 971 33 34 74
thegiricafe.com
→ p. 16 Ⓕ

5/Santa Eulària

Atzaró Spa
Carretera Sant Joan,
km 15
+34 971 33 88 38
atzaro.com
→ p. 20 Ⓞ

Bambuddha Grove
Carretera de Sant
Joan, km 8.5
+34 971 19 75 10
bambuddha.com
→ p. 31 Ⓕ

Bar Anita
Lugar Barri Sant
Carles, Sant Carles de
Peralta
+34 971 33 50 90
→ p. 16, 19 Ⓝ

dub

BE GOOD
TO YOU

DUB MAGAZINE - SPIRIT OF IBIZA
WWW.DUBIBIZA.COM

Bar Costa
Plaça de l'Església,
Santa Gertrudis
de Fruitera
+34 971 19 70 21
→ p. 31 Ⓕ

Bar Es Canto
Plaça de l'Església,
Santa Gertrudis
de Fruitera
→ p. 31 Ⓕ

Ca'n Pere Mussona
Carretera Santa
Eularia–Sant Carles,
km 9.3
+34 679 445 852
canperemussona.com
→ p. 32 Ⓢ

Can Caus
Carretera Santa
Gertrudis, km 3.5
+34 971 19 75 16
cancaus-ibiza.com
→ p. 21, 31 Ⓕ

Can Muson
Es Coloms, Santa
Eulària des Riu
+34 971 33 80 57
ibizacanmuson.com
→ p. 32 Ⓢ

Cas Pagés
Carretera Sant Carles,
km 10
+34 971 31 90 29
caspages.es
→ p. 21 Ⓕ

El Bigotes
Cala Mastella
+34 650 79 76 33
→ p. 11 Ⓕ

Es Caliu
Carretera Sant Joan,
km 10.8
+34 971 32 50 75
escaliuibiza.com
→ p. 21 Ⓕ

Las Dalias
Carretera Santa
Eulària–Sant Carles,
km 12
+34 971 32 68 25
lasdalias.es
→ p. 50 Ⓢ

Mercat Santa Eularia
Carrer del Sol, Santa
Eulària des Riu
+34 650 82 31 28
→ p. 32 Ⓢ

Restaurante Can Pau
Carretera Sant Miquel,
km 2.7
+34 971 19 70 07
→ p. 50 Ⓕ

Sant Carles de Peralta
(village)
→ p. 14 Ⓞ

Ses Escoles
Carretera Ibiza–
Portinatx, km 9.8
+34 871 87 02 29
canmiquelguasch.com
→ p. 20 Ⓕ

Sluiz
Carretera Santa
Gertrudis, km 3.5
+34 971 93 12 06
sluizibiza.com
→ p. 19 Ⓢ

Tetra Ibiza
Carretera Ibiza-San
Joan, km 12.9
→ p. 14 Ⓒ

The Rose
Venda de Fruitera, 2,
Santa Gertrudis de
Fruitera
→ p. 19 Ⓢ

6/Formen-
tera

Beso Beach
Playa de Cavall d'en
Borràs, Parque Natural
de Ses Salines
+34 971 32 45 72
→ p. 24 Ⓕ

Available from LOST iN

Next Issue: Lisbon

The Siren of Es Cavallet

Julio Herranz

When Alberto came home around seven, his mother always said the same. "So much sun isn't good for you, son; you'll end up a dried tuna. All that beach, beach, beach..." She'd scurry into the kitchen grumbling while the boy, paying no attention, went for a shower.

"And his dad will blame me... I was the one who insisted getting him the motorbike. But the boy was so excited, after the stress of his exams... Ay, it's so painful when they grow up. The day you least expect it they get married and then, we're alone again..."

When Alberto finally sat down his mother was still mumbling and preparing the eggs and chips. This had been the habitual menu for two weeks—lately he couldn't touch meat, let alone fish. "He's being strange, this boy. Something's up, Albertito, that's for sure. I'll find out what it is."

Strange? He thought he was acting normal, and was put out by his mother's suspicions. But how could she know? He'd sworn not to tell a soul. 'I have powers to find out,' she'd said, over and over. "If you ever tell anyone, you'll never see me again..."

He felt totally unhinged. Sometimes he'd wake up at night, out of his mind, shrieking "Escila, don't leave me!"

It all began a few days after finding her hideaway. He'd never been to Es Cavallet beach before. His mother would turn purple if a friend mentioned it. "It's an embarrassment. Those pigs should get naked at home and not in front of kids and decent people. Where will all this lead?" So he'd avoided upsetting his mother. At first, he'd stop at the top of the beach on the right. There was sand and the water was cleaner. But the atmosphere... There weren't many girls—it was mostly weird-looking men. They'd stare and he'd get nervous. So he decided to find a quieter spot where he could lie naked in peace. Finally, he found it—past the restaurant, behind the rocks. It was difficult to get down there, so it was always empty. With his radio, a snack and a bottle of water, Alberto could spread himself out in peace.

One day he'd fallen asleep, the radio was off and the only sound was the murmur of the sea among the rocks. He was woken by a soft, sweet voice, singing a mournful song of love. When he opened his eyes he froze. A siren sat there on her tail, in the classic posture. His first thought was some crazy woman was looking for attention. But the siren softly told him her story. And Alberto could prove it with his eyes—and hands. There was no doubt about it.

"Who'd have thought sirens existed? People will think I'm crazy."

"We rarely let ourselves be seen. People are cruel. They'd chain us up in a circus, or worse. You seem like a good boy. I've been watching you for a few days from the water, as you swam naked. I felt sad you were always alone. So we can be friends. But we only meet here. Nobody else can see us. And just a few hours each time. Deal? I'm Escila, you?"

Neither missed a single day. They connected on a magical level. Alberto would sit, dazed, listening to Escila's incredible stories. Tales of past centuries, fabulous adventures in which heroes were always guardians of innocence and hope. Everything was a happy dream: the noisy world beyond the rocks faded from existence. Time was suspended... Until the sad moment Escila disappeared once again under the waves.

They gave each other gifts. She brought him a gorgeous shell, like mother of pearl, whispering music like the echo of her voice. He gave a gold chain that the thrilled siren drew around her slippery waist.

One morning Alberto arrived at the beach to meet her. He was late as his mother had sent him on a few chores. But as he locked up his bike, he observed a commotion on the beach nearby. A mass of people crowded together babbling, waving arms wildly. Though he was in a hurry, he couldn't help his curiosity. He went down to see.

It was a gigantic fish—a deep-sea species he'd never seen before. What had such a creature been doing so close in? Obviously, it was dead. And sticking out of it was a fishing harpoon with the rope torn off. "Poor animal, what it must have suffered," he thought. He was about to slope away when one boy grabbed a stick and turned the beast over. As it rolled away from the dried seaweed, a ray of sunlight glinted off something—a golden chain.

Alberto couldn't contain himself. He shoved through the people and threw himself upon the giant fish. He hugged it and screamed in an uncontrollable bout of hysteria.

'Escila, my siren! My friend! What have they done to you? Murderers!'

There was a moment of silence before the crowd reacted.

Julio Herranz is an award-winning Cádiz-born poet and writer who has lived in Ibiza since 1974, working as cultural editor for local newspaper "Última Hora Ibiza" and publishing seven books to date

Illustration by Jonathan Niclaus

ON THE ROAD

The App for the Discerning Traveller

Explore insider recommendations and create your personal itinerary with handpicked locations tailored to your desires. Our selection of experiences ranges from independent boutiques, galleries, neighborhood bars to brand new restaurants. Experience a new city from within.

LOST iN